Encourage 2 Flourish

Robin Cook

Purpose Publishing
1503 Main Street #168
Grandview, Missouri
www.PurposePublishing.com

Copyright © 2018 Robin Cook
ISBN: 978-1-7326832-9-7
Book Cover Design by Robin Cook
Photographs and Interior Design by Robin Cook

No part of this publication may be reproduced, stored in retrieval system, or transmitted in any form or by any means, electronic, mechanical, photo copying, recording, scanning, or otherwise, except as permitted under Section 107 or 108 of the United States Copyright Act, without either the prior written permission of the Publisher.

Contact the author, Robin Cook, at www.Cook2Flourish.com for additional information and bulk pricing.

All scriptures contained in this book are referenced from
The Holy Bible, English Standard Version, The Holy Bible, New International Version, New King James Version of the Bible and the Holy Bible, New Living Translation.

Enjoy the variety of photos that feature God's beauty from Alaska, Kansas City, Fernandina Beach and other beautiful places! His splendor is all around us...

Printed in the United States of America.

ESV Bible
The ESV® Bible (The Holy Bible, English Standard Version®). ESV® Text Edition: 2016. Copyright © 2001 by Crossway, a publishing ministry of Good News Publishers. The ESV® text has been reproduced in cooperation with and by permission of Good News Publishers. Unauthorized reproduction of this publication is prohibited. All rights reserved.
The Holy Bible, English Standard Version (ESV) is adapted from the Revised Standard Version of the Bible, copyright Division of Christian Education of the National Council of the Churches of Christ in the U.S.A. All rights reserved.

New International Version
THE HOLY BIBLE, NEW INTERNATIONAL VERSION®, NIV® Copyright © 1973, 1978, 1984, 2011 by Biblica, Inc.™ Used by permission. All rights reserved worldwide.

New King James Bible
Scripture taken from the New King James Version®. Copyright © 1982 by Thomas Nelson. Used by permission. All rights reserved.

Holy Bible, New Living Translation, copyright © 1996, 2004, 2015 by Tyndale House Foundation. Used by permission of Tyndale House Publishers, Inc., Carol Stream, Illinois 60188. All rights reserved.

I will sing of the LORD'S great love forever; with my mouth I will make your faithfulness known through all generations. I will declare that your love stands firm forever, that you have established your faithfulness in heaven itself.
Psalm 89:1-2 NIV

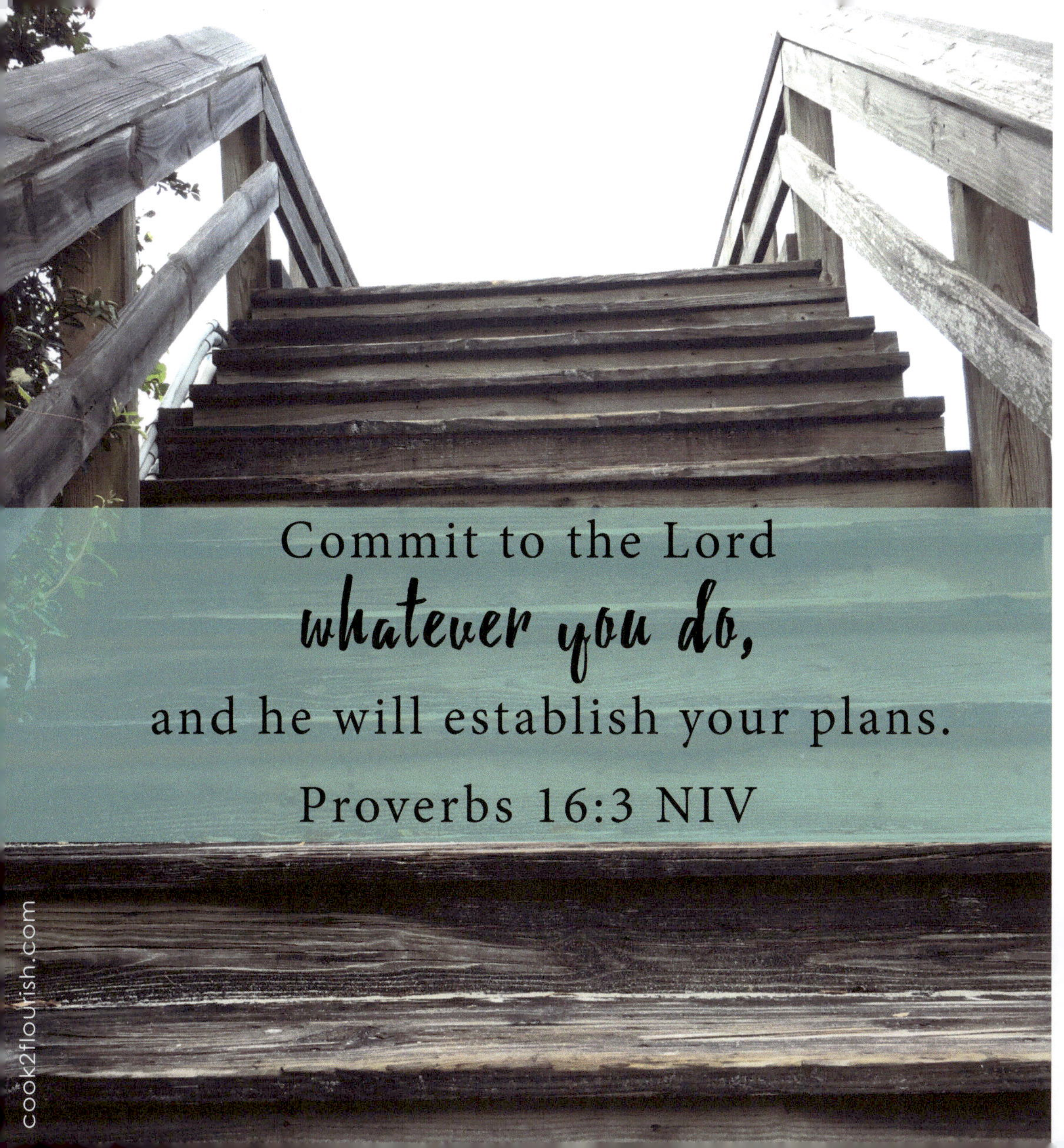
Commit to the Lord
whatever you do,
and he will establish your plans.
Proverbs 16:3 NIV
cook2flourish.com

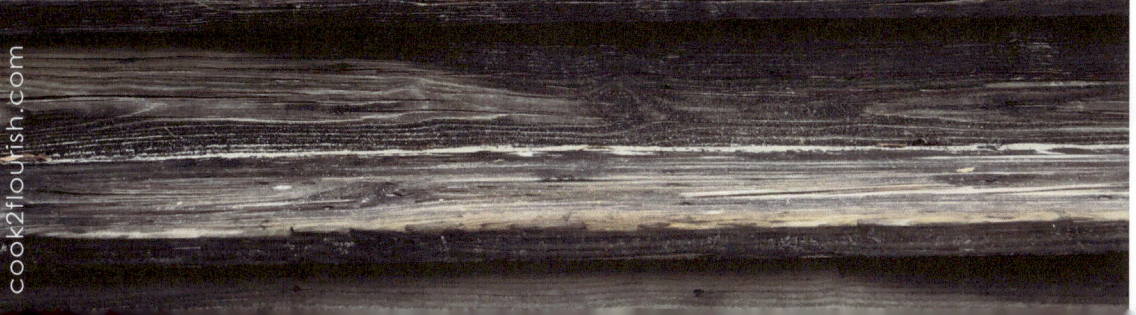

We continually ask God
to FILL you with the KNOWLEDGE of his will
through all the WISDOM and UNDERSTANDING that
the Spirit gives, so that you may
LIVE a life worthy of the Lord and
PLEASE him in every way:
bearing FRUIT in every good work,
GROWING in the knowledge of God,
being STRENGTHENED with all power
according to his glorious might
so that you may have great
ENDURANCE and PATIENCE.

Colossians 1:9b-11 NIV

cook2flourish.com

"*Be* strong and courageous. Do not be afraid or terrified because of them, for the Lord your God goes with you; he will never leave you nor forsake you."

DEUTERONOMY 31:6 NIV

cook2flourish.com

This is how God showed his love among us: He sent his one and only Son into the world that we might live through him. This is love: not that we loved God, but that he loved us and sent his Son as an atoning sacrifice for our sins.

1 John 4:9-10 NIV

Give all your worries and cares to God, for he cares about you.

I Peter 5:7 NLT

cook2flourish.com

Be on your guard; stand firm in the faith; be courageous; be strong. Do everything in love.

1 Corinthians 16:13-14 NIV

cook2flourish.com

THE *generous* SOUL WILL BE MADE RICH, AND HE WHO *waters* WILL ALSO BE WATERED HIMSELF... THE FRUIT OF THE *righteous* IS A TREE OF LIFE, AND HE WHO *wins* SOULS IS WISE.

PROVERBS 11:25,30 NKJV

cook2flourish.com

O God,
You are my God;
Early will I seek You;
My soul
thirsts for You;
My flesh
longs for You
In a dry and thirsty land
Where there is no water.

So I have
looked for You
in the sanctuary,
To see Your power and
Your glory.

Because Your
lovingkindness
is better than life,
My lips shall
praise You.

Psalm 63:1-3 NKJV

cook2flourish.com

The LORD is near to the brokenhearted
and saves the crushed in spirit.
Many are the afflictions of the righteous,
but the LORD delivers him out of them all.
Psalm 34:18-19 ESV

cook2flourish.com

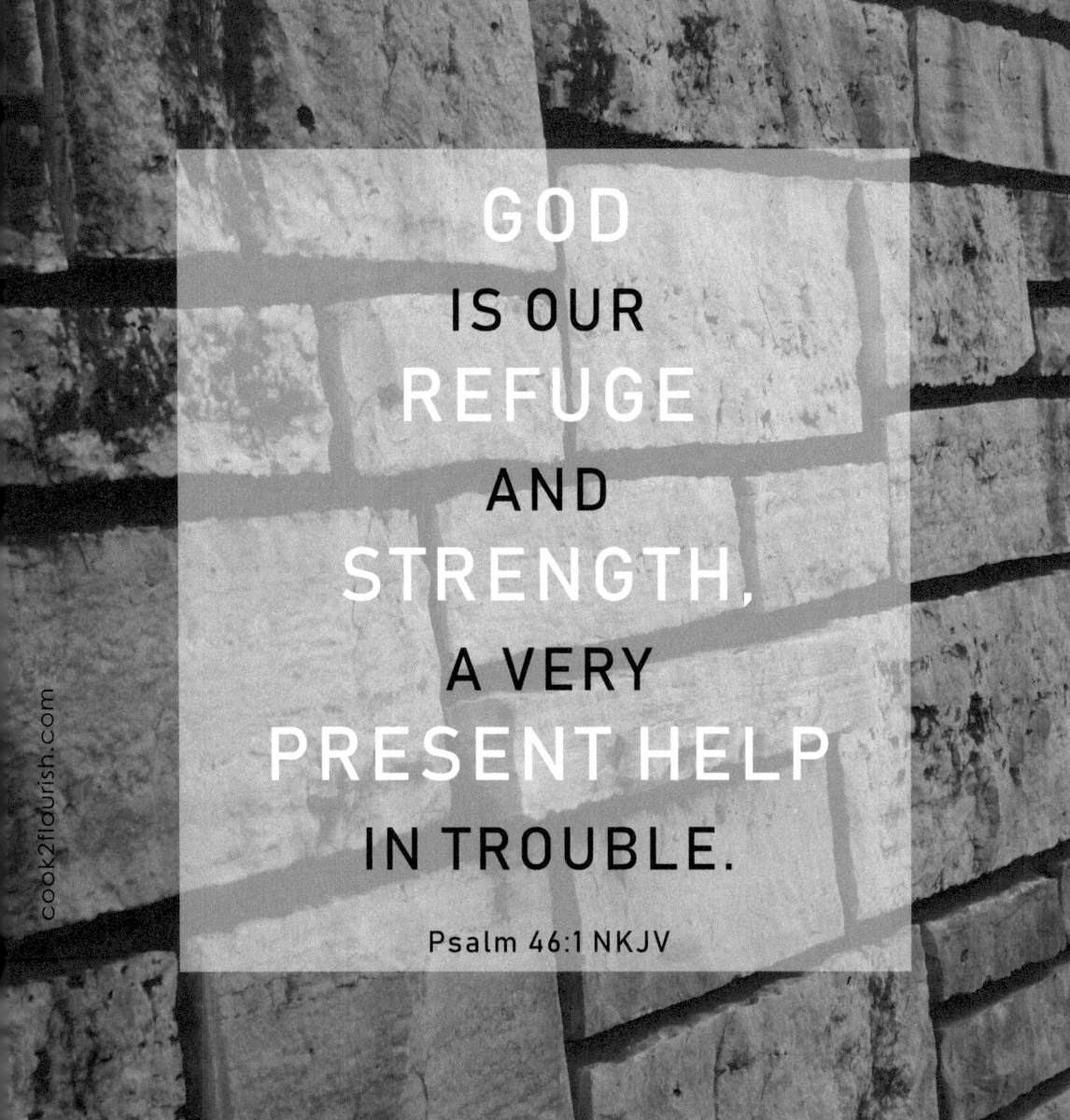

Blessed

be the God and Father
of our Lord Jesus Christ,
the Father of mercies and
God of all comfort,
who comforts us
in all our tribulation,
that we may be able to comfort
those who are in any trouble,
with the comfort with which we
ourselves are comforted by God.

2 Corinthians 1:3-4 NKJV

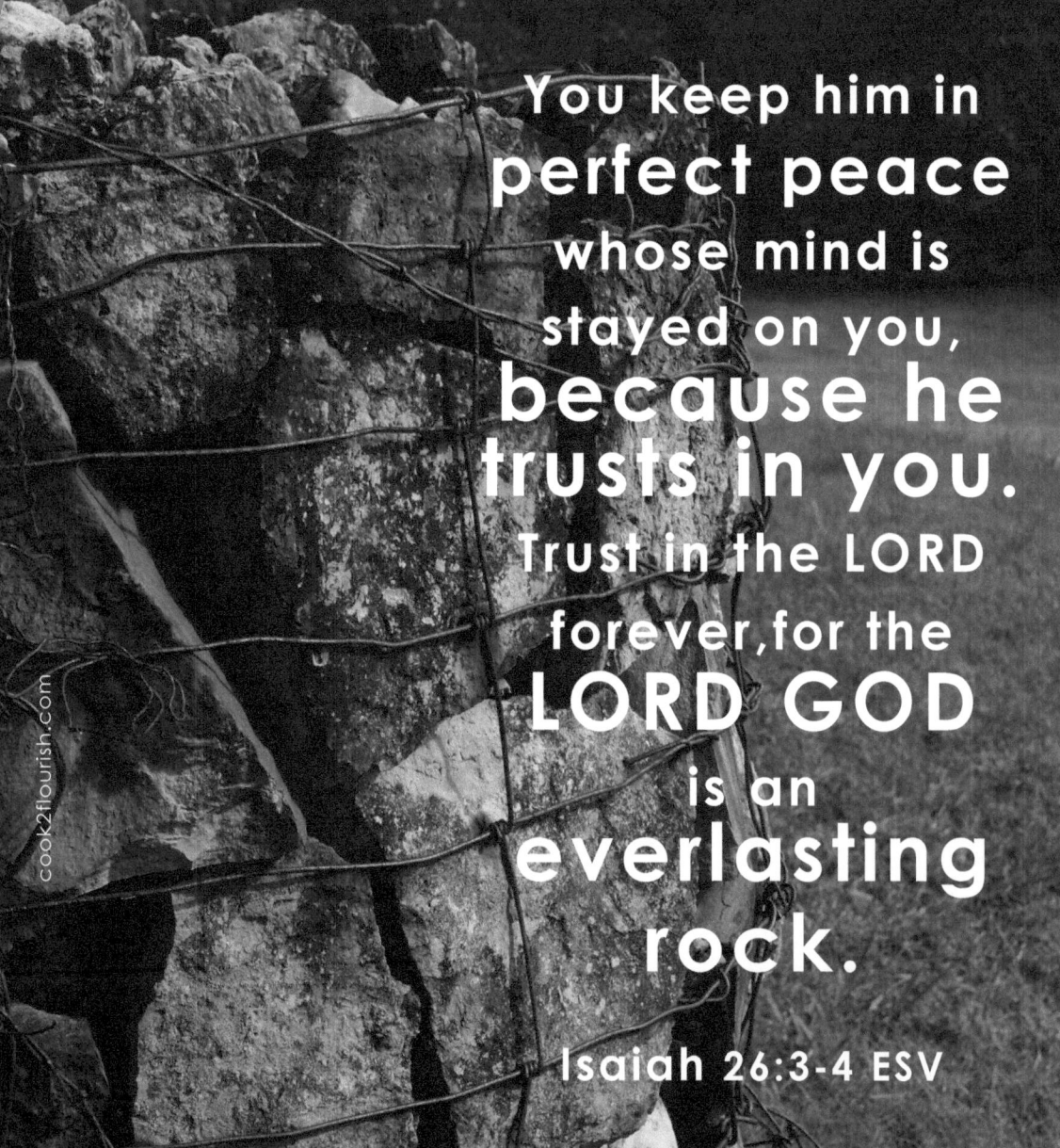

Then I will go to
the altar of God,

To God my
exceeding joy...

Why are you cast down,
O my soul?
And why are you
disquieted within me?

Hope in God;
For I shall yet praise
Him,
The help of my
countenance and my God.

Psalm 43:4a,5 NKJV

cook2flourish.com

Whoever confesses that
Jesus is the Son of God,
God abides in him,
and he in God.
So we have come
to know and
to believe
the love that God has for us.

GOD IS LOVE,

and whoever abides in love
abides in God,
and God abides in him...
There is no fear in love, but

PERFECT LOVE CASTS OUT FEAR...

We love because

HE FIRST LOVED US.

cook2flourish.com

BUT THANKS BE TO GOD!
HE GIVES US THE VICTORY
THROUGH OUR LORD JESUS CHRIST.
THEREFORE, MY DEAR BROTHERS AND SISTERS,
STAND FIRM. LET NOTHING MOVE YOU.
ALWAYS GIVE YOURSELVES FULLY
TO THE WORK OF THE LORD,
BECAUSE YOU KNOW THAT
YOUR LABOR IN THE LORD IS NOT IN VAIN.
1 CORINTHIANS 15:57- 58 NIV

Your eyes saw my substance,
being yet unformed.
And in Your book they all were written,
The days fashioned for me,
When as yet there were none of them.

How precious also are
Your thoughts to me, O God!
How great is the sum of them!
If I should count them,
they would be more in number
than the sand;

When I awake, I am still with You.
Psalm 139:16-18 NKJV

...let us strip off every weight
that slows us down,
especially the sin that so easily trips us up.
And let us run with endurance the race
God has set before us.
We do this by
keeping our eyes on Jesus,
the champion who
initiates and perfects our faith.
Because of the joy awaiting him,
he endured the cross, disregarding its shame.
Now he is seated in the place of honor
beside God's throne.

cook2flourish.com

And let us not grow weary of doing good, for in due season we will reap, if we do not give up.

Galatians 6:9 ESV

cook2flourish.com

but those who
hope in the LORD
will renew their strength.
They will soar
on wings like eagles;
they will run and
not grow weary,
they will walk and not be faint.
Isaiah 40:31 NIV

It is God who arms me with strength, And makes my way perfect.

Psalm 18:32 NKJV

cook2flourish.com

...God has said,
"Never will I leave you;
never will I forsake you."
So we say
with confidence,

"The Lord is my helper;
I will not be afraid.
What can mere mortals
do to me?"...

Jesus Christ is the same
yesterday and
today and
forever.

Hebrews 13:5b-6,8 NIV

cook2flourish.com

encourage daily...
pray continually

Heavenly Father, please give these dear ones grace, peace and spiritual insight that they may flourish daily in relationship with You through Christ Jesus...
Hebrews 3:13, 1 Thessalonians 5:17 NIV, Ephesians 1:2,17

cook2flourish.com

Love:
Psalm 63:1-3 NKJV
Psalm 89:1-2 NIV
1 Corinthians 16:13-14 NIV
1 John 4:9-10 NIV
1 John 4:15-16,18a,19 ESV

Joy:
Psalm 16:11 NKJV
Psalm 43:4a,5 NKJV

Peace:
Psalm 46:1 NKJV
Isaiah 26:3-4 ESV
Hebrews 13:5b-6,8 NIV

Hope:
Psalm 25:4-5 NIV
Psalm 43:4a,5 NKJV
Psalm 119:114, 151 NIV
Isaiah 40:31 NIV

Comfort:
Psalm 34:17-19 ESV
Psalm 138:7-8 NKJV
2 Corinthians 1:3-4 NKJV

God's Faithfulness:
Hebrews 13:5b-6,8 NIV
Psalm 89:1-2 NIV

Purpose:
Psalm 25:4-5 NIV
Psalm 139:16-18 NKJV
Colossians 1:9b-11 NIV
Hebrews 12:B1-2 NLT

Wisdom for life:
Psalm 16:11 NKJV
Psalm 25:4-5 NIV
Proverbs 3:5-6 NLT
Proverbs 16:3 NIV
Colossians 1:9b-11 NIV

Victory in Christ:
1 Corinthians 15:57-58 NIV

Courage:
Psalm 34:4-5 NIV
Psalm 55:22 ESV
1 Corinthians 16:13-14 NIV

Overwhelmed/Fear:
Deuteronomy 31:6 NIV
Psalm 55:22 ESV
1 Peter 5:7 NLT
1 John 4:15-16,18a,19 ESV

Living Fruitfully:
Proverbs 11:25,30 NKJV
Galatians 6:9 ESV
Colossians 1:9b-11 NIV

Generosity:
Proverbs 11:25,30 NKJV

Spiritual Endurance:
1 Corinthians 15:57-58 NIV
Galatians 6:9 ESV
Hebrews 12:B1-2 NLT

Strength
Psalm 18:32 NKJV
Psalm 46:1 NKJV
Psalm 73:25-26 ESV
Isaiah 40:31 NIV
1 Corinthians 16:13-14 NIV
Colossians 1:9b-11 NIV

Health:
Psalm 73:25-26 ESV
Psalm 103:2-3 NKJV

Prayers of the Heart:
Psalm 25:4-5 NIV
Psalm 63:1-3 NKJV
Colossians 1:9b-11 NIV

The most beautiful display of love the world has ever seen, Jesus Christ, the Creator King, came and died for you and me. Despite our sins, flaws and shortcomings that created a chasm between the holiness of God and humanity, Jesus humbled Himself and took on flesh. He dwelt on the earth He created, knowing the price He'd need to pay with His precious blood.

Motivated by love, He graciously paid our soul's debt so we could be forgiven and free. Jesus paid it all- there is no sin too great or soul too far- Jesus proved it by His scars. His dripping blood poured out in love is the only way we can be accepted into heaven above. His hand can be seen in each painted sky and all creation far and wide.

Personally He asks, "Will you come unto Me? I alone can set your soul free, enable you to be all I've created you to be, and have a relationship with you now through eternity."

Your soul was costly, but worth it...

Your sin made a stain, but I cleansed it...

Your heart was dead, but I was resurrected to revive it...

If you believe in Me, you will not die, but live eternally...

Eternal life is knowing Me, Jesus Your loving Savior King.

(John 3:16-17, 17:3)

cook2flourish.com

Dear Friend,

Thank you so much for the opportunity to share these Scriptures with you and with those God brings into your life! God's Word is so powerful, and I'm so grateful how He continues to transform my life as I study it. As you read these cards, may you be encouraged, spiritually invigorated and compelled to share this eternally beneficial truth. God's Word endures forever, and encouragement is always needed in every day of our lives.

Let's daily decide to abide in Christ by reading the Bible or simply saying, "Jesus, I need You today, have your way in my life and use me to shine your light to the people in my life today. Help me to speak your truth with grace and salt that others may be encouraged and inspired to seek You..."

As you draw near to God, He will draw near to you like His Word promises in James 4:8. In heaven it will be indescribably amazing to hear how Jesus worked through you to be a blessing to those around you. Eternity is near... Let's encourage 2 flourish for the glory of Christ Jesus!

With Joy,
Robin Cook

cook2flourish.com

www.ingramcontent.com/pod-product-compliance
Lightning Source LLC
Chambersburg PA
CBHW041113070526
44584CB00002B/151